PRAISE FOR *RURAL EDUCATION*

I admire these poems for their precision and the attention they pay to rural life. Anyone who has lived in one of these places can relate to the sense of connection and disconnection from the larger activities of American life. We feel the matter-of-fact mortality of the living things around us. If you are not from these places, these poems bring you there with carefully chosen details—textures, colors, plants, and everyday objects. These, like the people who appear in the poems, are presented without judgment or romanticism. Altogether, *Rural Education* asks questions about toxicity, about beauty, about memory and nostalgia. It's brutally, darkly, comically real.

    —Charles Malone,
      author of *Working Hypothesis* and *Questions About Circulation*

Rural Education is full of unexpected solace, violence, and childhood desire set in a "mostly ag" town. There are rural elegies, yes, and plainspoken work poems whose startling images sometimes rise as extravagances from the "mudcake" landscape. But what I appreciate most is that in every failing clutch and taciturn engine, in every bloated heifer, mowed-over prairie toad, and rabid skunk is a tender excavation of rural masculinity and the anxieties of being human.

    —Elyse Fenton,
      author of *Clamor* and *Sweet Insurgent*

With precise language that haunts with its careful specificity, these poems evoke not just a place but a range of feelings in a way that feels wholly original, where memory is "like a museum diorama/set east of sagebrush and foothills." Even if you've never lived in a rural place "strung out along the main drag," any reader who has tried to reconcile how where they came from shaped who they are, or who has looked in the mirror and seen more of their parents than themselves, will be transfixed by these poems. I know I was.

    —Susan Leslie Moore,
      author of *That Place Where You Opened Your Hands*

Propelled by its steady cadences, crystalline images, and plainspoken music, *Rural Education* distills the entire essence of a boy's coming of age in these acutely observed poems. Each memory lands with consequence, via writing that's clear and hard as glass—whether it's the crackle of AM radio, riding bikes everywhere and nowhere, mowing miles of fried-up crabgrass, or the jolt and shudder of learning to drive stick in a '67 El Camino. Schneider has crafted a transporting gem, one with the full arc and ache of a novel, capturing the beauty, loneliness, and wonder of a free-range childhood in this deceptively slender collection.

    —Michael Bazzett,
      author of *Cloudwatcher, The Popol Vuh, The Echo Chamber,* and *The Temple*

Rural Education

poems by

Evan P. Schneider

Finishing Line Press
Georgetown, Kentucky

Rural Education

ACKNOWLEDGMENTS

My deepest appreciation for those willing to read and discuss countless
versions of these poems and this short collection as it took shape over the
years including Michael Matson, Judith Edwards, Kjerstin Johnson,
Heather Brown, Mike Datz, Mike Bernhardt, Andrew Bohn, Shea'la Finch,
Martha Grover, Justin Hocking, Michael Heald, Jay Clarke, Jessie Carver,
and Bruce Snider.

For their longstanding literary friendship, I am indebted to Dan DeWeese,
Mary Rechner, Lucas Bernhardt, Kjerstin Johnson, Lysley Tenorio,
Satya Doyle Byock, and Charlie Malone.

And thank you to the publications in which some of these poems previously
appeared in slightly different forms, including *Rattle* ("Rural Education
II," a finalist for the 2024 *Rattle* Poetry Prize), *Moonstone Arts Center 2024
Freedom Anthology* ("Independence Day"), and *CrayfishMag* ("Rural
Education" and "Memories of Some Consequence").

Publisher: Leah Huete de Maines
Editor: Christen Kincaid
Cover Art: *Landscape* by Circle of Carl Rottmann, in public domain
Cover Design: Elizabeth Maines McCleavy

Order online: www.finishinglinepress.com
also available on amazon.com

Author inquiries and mail orders:
Finishing Line Press
PO Box 1626
Georgetown, Kentucky 40324
USA

Contents

Boy's Life 1

CBS News Sunday Morning with Charles Kuralt 2

Severe Weather Possible for Weld County 3

Work Experience 4

Rural Education 5

Late 20th-Century Siblings & A Queensland Blue Heeler 7

Rural Education II 8

Independence Day 9

Youth Sports 10

Boy's Life II 11

Memories of Some Consequence 12

Peeling Potatoes 14

Small-Town Politics 15

Rural Education III 16

Work Experience II 17

Boy's Life III 18

Work Experience III 19

Driving Home on the Highway After Being Away for Some Time .. 21

Bygones 22

Nowadays 23

Bygones II 25

On Seeing the Union Pacific from a Freeway Overpass Today 26

Notes, etc. 28

Of all your hopes, your dissolving endeavors
To keep close track
Of who you are, and where you had started from,
and why
—David Wagoner

BOY'S LIFE

Twelve years old and I make a habit
of running down the graveled-over
driveway itching with anticipation

awaiting the arrival any day
of the mail-order camouflage
buck knife I bought myself

advertised in the scouting mag
shipped from Baton Rouge
someplace I somehow knew

I'd never visit but loved to
pronounce in clueless wonder
bat-on-roo-zha, ba-TON rooj.

A gnarly thing with a hollow plastic
handle stuffed with a space blanket
a tight roll of ultra-tough twine

and eight waterproof matches.
Its swiveling compass end and
matte-black *Rambo*-esque blade

swooped and sharp on one side
serrated on the other: for what
I wasn't ever sure. Sending $11.99

plus S&H, check I asked my mom
to write, told to make it out myself
right then and there was the start

a lifelong routine of wanting something
I didn't understand and didn't need
dangerous as it might be.

CBS NEWS SUNDAY MORNING
WITH CHARLES KURALT

Dad calls us to the family room
so we mosey in and plop down
for the three-minute nature scene
at the end of every broadcast.
Mist rises from tall brown grass
cricket chirp echoes in the azure
morning ether, a red-tailed hawk
lands in a sickly cottonwood.
Another hawk off screen lets out a hoarse
keeeeeeeeee-arr, then others join in kind
a killdeer, a robin, gnats bobbing in the
sunrise. Just like that it's over, bald truth-
telling host saying something like
look for the joy in your life, look closely
and often. It's not always so easy to find.

SEVERE WEATHER POSSIBLE
FOR WELD COUNTY

I'm at the house alone
mom and sister at softball
dad down in Denver. That time

of day clear skies close up purple
at the edges of the afternoon and
news interrupts *The Dukes of*

Hazzard, electronic caw-caw-caw.
Tornado watch or warning, it's
all the same to dark roiling clouds

so I sprint to the crawl space and stay
hidden for hours, praying not to be
trapped in an earthen hole

below my small, short life
not knowing how many wolf
spiders and snakes seek solace

down there too, survival
made moot by the minute
already underground.

WORK EXPERIENCE

Mowing miles of fried-up crabgrass
prairie toad I didn't see until it was
too late, double-bladed mulching mower

unwieldy for my dull and choppy mind
guessing between brake and throttle.
Walking the quarter mile home

without finishing the work, choke-
cherries hung in the culvert trees
distracting me from the deed

and staining my fingers and mouth
whatever blood-red color that was
whatever color it's faded to since.

RURAL EDUCATION

Rabid skunks cozy up in doghouses
when your father's out of town.
It's midnight, a middle school year
and your mother says she needs you,
look at her, needs you to help out.
The neighbor's come up, an off-duty
deputy, and puts a pistol in your hand
guiding you to take aim in the dark
like an orange, go ahead now son
just slowly squeeze the trigger.
Middle of that next morning
middle of that sad hot summer
and no one shows you the way
to shovel skunk off dark internal walls
but you learn why and how
long that stench will last.

LATE 20TH-CENTURY SIBLINGS
& A QUEENSLAND BLUE HEELER

After Alfred Bailey, Denver Museum of Nature & Science

Memory like a museum diorama
set east of sagebrush and foothills.
Under a washed-out cloud-blotched sky
a family dog, a cattle dog, *Canis lupus
familiaris* waits to give snarl-lipped chase
daily life captured *in medias res*
blue heeler protecting our country yard
from us, two kids at a chain-link gate
emptied-out school bus in the background
runaway road like soiled yarn knitted deep
into the grassed-over mudcake landscape
life's ur-story unspooling from there.

RURAL EDUCATION II

When my classmate's cow died
in the name of science they winched it

onto the junior high football field just as
the sky started to spit small white pellets

so we gathered round the bloated heifer, hands
deep in our pockets, chins tucked to our chests

to watch our biology teacher perform
an autopsy. Not to determine the cause

of death, but to show us the warm insides
of something so recently alive, how the body

works, or doesn't. Things take a weird turn
when George, twice as big as any other kid

without warning grabs one of the eyeballs
off the bloody tarp and puts it in his mouth

cutting the lesson short, or rather changing it
into a different one about humans and how

they'll do anything for attention, anything for love
showing you how much they're hurting or lonely

or both, that toxic concoction of being scared
of everything, and nothing, then being taught

to hide it, hide it as long and as well as you can.

INDEPENDENCE DAY

Mostly ag town strung out along the main drag
smell of fire hydrant water on hot concrete

yellow and cherry-red firetrucks parading
firefighters tossing candy to us kids.

Riding bikes everywhere, nowhere, farmhouse
to farmhouse until the car show's finished and

we pull up bottomed-out lawn chairs next to our
tired and tipsy parents draining cans of Coors

as they face the coming twilight. Fireworks sprout
slowly like they're far off even if they're not until

the sheriff turns on his lights, says we best be
getting home and we do, us kids swerving on

two wheels between Roman candle bursts
showing off our wheelie ride, our bunny hop

what we wouldn't do for another lap around
the schoolyard, another lap on a summer night

as that once-a-year sulfur tinge lingers in the air.

YOUTH SPORTS

The theory was
if you could win
with subpar
equipment

you were stronger
and it meant more
than for other kids
with Air Jordans.

The reality was
if you could win
it was likely due to
your determination

not to draw attention
to yourself, your size
or your second-tier
multi-sport shoes.

BOY'S LIFE II

Mud-bubbled swallows' nests
brought down skipping rocks
off ditch bridge undersides
spanning the heavy stream
of milk-silt irrigation water
rolling fast and hard.

Same muddy trench my school
friend drowned in, caught two
feet under on the iron-runged sieve
before he even knew he slipped
hours before anyone wondered
when he'd be coming home.

MEMORIES OF SOME CONSEQUENCE

After Erika L. Sánchez

Summer morning bike rides to play a borrowed baritone.
Two-player cheat codes and the whole afternoon.
Rows and rows of useless shit: Fridays at the farm town auction.
Hee Haw laugh track, steak dinners on TV trays.
Dead buck next to a barbed wire fence, one clean cut to the throat.
Emmylou Harris LPs spinning on Sunday mornings.
Hoping to glimpse a nipple on HBO.
The easy pass of wine coolers on weekend afternoons.
Running up for a gulp of Pepsi, learning it's an ash can.
Making out behind the junior high until everyone's lips are raw.
Voice of Al Michaels narrating *Monday Night Football*.
Discussing guns at Christmas, the year Santa brought mom a toaster.
Climbing atop the Lions Club, the sheriff yelling at us from his car.
Realizing the magazine in black plastic was full of naked women.
School-sanctioned roller-skating to the beats of Jon Bon Jovi.

PEELING POTATOES

The way my mother
used to peel potatoes

leaning over the sink
garbage disposal going

brownish hair blonding
from altitude and sun

cutting toward herself
an apple of the earth

skin curling off little
by little. As I watch

now she heaps
several spoonfuls

of sugar into cups of
early-morning coffee

takes walks to smoke
a cigarette or three

and who am I to argue?
Dusty garden she defended

from miller moths and rabbits
tank-topped and sunburned

raking and re-raking our
reclaimed patch of rented range

same color as her summer hair.

SMALL-TOWN POLITICS

Iridescent grackles
    those so-called invasive
        common blue-black birds

remind me of my dad
    and his 12-gauge resting
        by the front door ready

for him to step out
    onto the cluttered porch
        at a moment's notice and shoot

them one by one out of the aging elms.
    Grackles, he says, steal other birds' nests
        eat their eggs and don't belong here anyway.

So he "dissuades" them
    shot after shot ringing out
        over the mute, dun prairie

no one near enough
    to care or question
        the tiny explosions

of black and blue plumage
    shimmering in the dusky light
        before he heads inside to catch the nightly news.

RURAL EDUCATION III

Learning to drive stick in the field
behind our house, night after night
in a '67 El Camino that needed a
new battery, needed to be jumped
every time I stalled it—every try
of course. We begin at sundown
super moon coming up tawny
behind the eastern prairie hills
me at the wheel, dad alongside
arm on the rolled-down window
as I kill it again and again and
always get the same advice:
easy does it on the throttle
let that clutch out slowly.

WORK EXPERIENCE II

Mowing miles of fertilized bluegrass
on manicured corporate campuses

of HP, AB, Teledyne Waterpik
I'm by far the least experienced

in the ways of the world of everyone
in my crew, three of us crammed

on the company truck bench seat
a rough guy with a chiseled leather

face in his 50s, his makeshift
sidekick, a tough guy in his 20s who

wears Semper Fi t-shirts and chews
his plastic Frosty straw down to a nub

on our half-hour Wendy's break
one day asking me what I prefer

kine bud or big bud? I said I'd never
even had a beer. You know what I mean

right?! Jesus how old am I anyway?
What am I a pussy? What am I indeed

but a straight-edge kid with swaths to learn
blades of grass stuck to my face via SPF 30

slathered on at oh-six hundred
and religiously reapplied.

BOY'S LIFE III

Football game broadcasts
on the crackly AM radio

cicada sound of a crowd
in some distant, colder city

like Buffalo two time zones ahead.
We're operating on a choked-up

carburetor again, common rural
vivisection, on an old dog food bag

protecting the sacred driveway
from errant oil drips. Waning

equinox light holds
two and two together

aspen tree's gold coins jangle
quietly out front of the house

prop plane putters overhead
dog barking in the distance

contrail like a bony zipper
down the center of the sky.

Night comes and inside on the TV
Al Bundy laughs cruelly at his wife

and you promise yourself one day
you'll never do the same, but some

things follow you forever, don't they
like shadows you never squarely see.

WORK EXPERIENCE III

Weekend nights, acne and all, making dough
    tossing pies at the pizza place, serving up

soft-serve sugar cones: vanilla, chocolate, or twist?
    Sometimes it got up to 130, working with my crush

from 5th grade beside my best friend's girlfriend
    both of whom would be women soon

and had experiences they'd rather not
    talk about. Our boss died in a head-on

not long after he'd worked past midnight
    singing along with us to the *Pulp Fiction*

soundtrack of those shifts, swapping lyrics like
    only one who could ever reach me

was the son of a pizza man. *C'est la vie*
    say the old folks, it just goes to show

you never can tell what you'll remember
    what you'll so willingly and easily forget.

DRIVING HOME ON THE HIGHWAY
AFTER BEING AWAY FOR SOME TIME

Cloud towers billow
    like gently used cotton balls
        glued on blue construction paper

crosshatched patches
    of beiges and taupes
        sprawled on the plain below.

Further on a BNSF
    half-mile train hoists
        its own brown column

that falls away in chugs
    and fades off into the flats.
        Near town the nimbostrati peter

into a shook-down
    series of cumulus plateaus.
        Someone's flicked cigarette

still smokes at the off-ramp
    as the AC tugs incessantly
        on the heated, tired engine.

Other drivers tailgate
    and signal impatiently
        possibly forgetting it's Sunday

and difficult to sit with that
    trapped-in feeling inherent
        to vast unprotected openness.

BYGONES

I see it from the overgrown driveway
in a half-fallen elm with missing limbs.
The faded plywood of my childhood
treehouse sags prairie-storm-battered
mostly blown away thirty years on
but my first thought is still to climb
the shaky leaning ladder I once built
listening to oldies on my Walkman.
Climb like I used to every summer morning
watching beet trucks fishtail and swerve
on the corners of sandy country roads:
one boy's view of the modern world
little more than a slumping platform
nailed with precision to a questionable tree.

NOWADAYS

Northeast of Virginia Dale two steam locomotives roll through Wyoming toward Utah, sesquicentennial commemoration of transcontinental railroading, terminus at Promontory Summit. My mother wears a blue coat and stands by the green gate next to a couple from town with whom she and my father trade small talk about winter, how it always tends to stick around. Part of a handful of plains folk gathered to glimpse the painted rebuilt past, clacking and puffing, inch by inch, riveted and plodding like the iron horse it is in this inglorious age of unicorns.

BYGONES II

That point you see your father's face
blinking back at you in the mirror
surprised when you see his body
as you dress yourself, same flannel
same ball cap and glasses, same style
of lacing up softened-leather boots.
Around that time you see your sister
in a photograph of your grandmother
as a little girl, and your mother's face
in a snapshot of your newborn niece.
Where this puts you now is anyone's
guess, somewhere between brown pastures
of youth and a forest of old-growth habits.

ON SEEING THE UNION PACIFIC FROM A FREEWAY OVERPASS TODAY

At this height
at this age and angle

train cars morph into replica
reminders of the half-finished

model hanging from the rafters
of my parents' packed garage

as far as we ever got in making
the world as I left it, small but

picturesque. Bluffs and trestle bridge
maples in miniature are proof enough

not every road's a through road
not everything started is finished.

After the dwarf hill beside the still
epoxy rivers, in-scene and tilt-shift

the track cants gently now
and its banked curves compel me:

take a low seat by the tiny conductor
and a long look around.

What needs building still
what needs demolishing?

NOTES, ETC.

Epigraph: David Wagoner. "Being Shot," *Poetry Magazine*, December 1975.

Page 2: Co-created by original host Charles Kuralt, *Sunday Morning* has aired on CBS since 1979. For most of its history, the program ended with a one- to three-minute non-narrated, untitled nature scene.

Page 7: Under the direction of Alfred Bailey, the Denver Museum of Nature & Science became home to 89 world-famous wildlife dioramas that feature carefully crafted reproductions of animals, plants, and flowers in front of finely painted backgrounds.

Page 12: Erika L. Sánchez. "Memories of No Consequence," *Poetry Magazine*, June 2024.

Evan P. Schneider's writing has appeared in *The Normal School*, *Rattle*, *CrayfishMag*, *McSweeney's*, and elsewhere. Author of the novel *A Simple Machine, Like the Lever* and founding editor of *Boneshaker: A Bicycling Almanac*, Schneider has received support for his work from the Oregon Arts Commission and Kimmel Harding Nelson Center for the Arts. Born and raised in the Southwest, Schneider now lives in Oregon. *Rural Education* is his first chapbook. Visit him online at *evanpschneider.com*.

www.ingramcontent.com/pod-product-compliance
Lightning Source LLC
Chambersburg PA
CBHW022057080426
42734CB00009B/1380